Wall of Water

by

Royal Flaxman

with Dean Parkin

D1439844

First Published 1993 by Rushmere Publishing
32 Rushmere Road, Carlton Colville, Lowestoft, Suffolk

Typeset by Anglia Repro Services
133 South Quay, Great Yarmouth, Norfolk

Printed in England by Blackwell Print & Design
133 South Quay, Great Yarmouth, Norfolk

ISBN 1 872992 07 2

Wall of Water

LOWESTOFT & OULTON BROAD
DURING THE 1953 FLOOD

by

Royal Flaxman

with Dean Parkin

Rushmere
Publishing

Acknowledgements

I would like to thank all those people who have contributed to this book and loaned photographs, especially, Peter Jenkins of Ford Jenkins photographers, Divisional Commander (Retired) Ron Bishop, Mrs I. Thorpe, Mrs S. C. Mitchell, Mr D. Hannant, Mr F. Rout, Mr M. Barnard, Mr J. W. A. Dann, Mr A. G. Wren, Mr C. Meeking, Mr J. Burt, Mr G. Blowers, Mr A. J. Meade, Mrs L. G. Rose, Mr P. Hemsley, Mr R. Parker, Mr V. I. Chipperfield, my publisher Dean Parkin and the proof readers, Bruce Parkin, Heather Parkin and Christine Johnson. Special thanks to J. Honeybone for permission to use the photograph of me on the back cover.

Finally I would like to thank Trevor Westgate of the Lowestoft Journal, Waveney District Council and BBC Radio Suffolk and everyone else who has contributed in some shape or form to this book.

A resident of one of the houses at the bottom of Herring Fishery Score checks the water level. It was impossible to tell how much damage was done to the houses by the flood water as much of it occurred in the foundations. Many are still scraping salt from the walls to this day.

The Bridge Road area where Royal affected the rescue of a taxi and its passengers.

Introduction

Over the last few months I have relived the flood of 1953 many times. I have been taken through the events of that night, through forty-year-old memories, which were recounted as if it were yesterday.

I too can remember that night. I was working for Shell UK as a lorry driver and that evening I was having a quiet drink in the *Lady of the Lake* hotel with my friend, Russell Graves. Suddenly Russell said, "I think the carpet behind the bar moved up and down!" There was water coming in under the door and beneath the carpet. We knew it was a high tide but we didn't expect what was to happen . . . .

We went out in the street and an absolute torrent of water was rushing around Waller's Restaurant and coming up the road fast to the *Lady of the Lake*. People started coming out of the various pubs and places in the area and we joined the gathering crowd which began to retreat in the direction of the Oulton Broad Post Office.

Then we saw a taxi which appeared to be in trouble having stalled in the water. It must have come over the bridge about the same time as the flood burst Lake Lothing's banks. I had to act fast. I got my lorry from the car park, put on my rubber boots and attached a tow rope to the back of the vehicle. I started her up and said to a special constable, "Get these people out the way and I'll go in and get them!" The crowd was moved back and I began to reverse into the water until I was a couple of yards away from the taxi, with its driver and two passengers looking pretty scared! As I wrapped my tow rope around the taxi's bumper, my rubber boots immediately filled with water, which was rising all the time and the force of it had begun to move the taxi sideways!

I drove up the road about fifty yards and suddenly realised that all the people were shouting at me. When I looked out the window I found that I'd left the taxi behind! Back I went and this time made certain that the rope was secure. Then my lorry wouldn't start and I had to urge her on, "Come on old girl! You can do it!" and thankfully she fired! Slowly we began to go forward, pulling the taxi behind us, until we were both clear of the water, receiving a big cheer from the watching crowd.

A forty-year-old thank you. At his flood exhibition in February 1993, Royal Flaxman met Ernest Martin, one of the passengers in the taxi that Royal rescued with his lorry.

Two years ago I met the daughter of the taxi driver, Sidney Stevenson, at one of my exhibitions and in February this year I received a phone call from Mr Ernest Martin who turned out to be one of the passengers in the taxi that evening! It seems he had heard me being interviewed on BBC Radio Suffolk about my 1993 flood exhibition that took place in February this year at Lowestoft Library.

This exhibition, along with letters from readers of the Lowestoft Journal, provided a substantial amount of the information for the story of the flood. The basis for this book though is the forty or so photographs that I took on the night of the flood and the following day in and around Lowestoft, a night that I and many others won't ever forget . . .!

ROYAL FLAXMAN

June 1993,
Lowestoft

The North Denes was still under water the next day. This photograph was taken from the lower gate of the Sparrow's Nest and shows the motor cycle, a Panther 350, which was the method of transport used to get about town to take photographs of the aftermath.

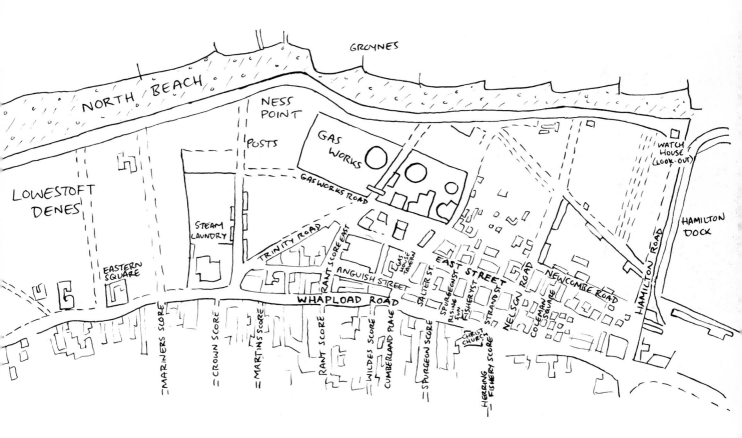

In the following pages there are frequent references to the Beach Village. The map above shows this area, which disappeared completely in the 1960s, demolished to make way for industry.

Taken by Royal himself, this picture showing the torrent near Waller's in Oulton Broad, is perhaps one of the most dramatic photographs of the flood. Royal remembers, ". . . Though the water was just knee high, the force of the current was such that it was difficult to keep your balance. In fact, I had to be steadied by Mr Buckley, son of *The Wherry's* proprietor at the time, in order to take this picture . . . ."

The Flood That Threatened

The cause of the 1953 flood was a cyclone which began in West Scotland then moved to the North Sea. This caused gusts of wind up to 113 mph which drove the sea southwards, combined with the usual high tides and resulted in the flooding of the East Coast and Lowestoft.

This however was not the first time that such a wind had caused flooding in the town. On Saturday, November 18th 1893, similar conditions wreaked havoc amongst the fishing fleet and destroyed part of the sea wall and cliff at Pakefield.

Lowestoft was flooded again four years later, on Sunday November 28th 1897, when "a tide as had never been known before," surged over the fish markets and flooded Commercial Road, Belvedere Road, the Royal Plain, while the London Road was flooded to a depth of a couple of feet for several yards.

It wasn't until Wednesday 25th November 1925 that the town witnessed severe flooding again though, when a record high tide of twenty-four feet was aided by a north-west wind and flooded Christchurch Plain and threatened to inundate the Church itself.

In February 1938 the same area was again flooded and also St. John's Street south of the bridge. Huge waves poured over the wall onto the pickling plots and surged down Hamilton Road along its whole length. Fortunately with a change of wind from north-west to north-east the water soon disappeared. In 1953 there would be no such good fortune . . ..

Huge waves crash into the Victoria Bathing Station on the Jubilee Parade. Note the railings, twisted and buckled by the force of the sea.

SECTION 1

"The Wall of Water"

The warnings were there. "My dad, Alec Waters, knew there was going to be a flood," remembers Mrs Smith, "He went down to the sea with his wellies, socks pulled over the top, a big duffel coat on and when he came back he said, 'There's going to be a flood, you'd better get some supplies in.' So my mother went out to get some paraffin, meths, food, and we were all geared up for the emergency."

Although a fisherman like Mr Waters might have realised the significance of severe north-westerly gales combined with spring tides, few could have foreseen that January 31st 1953 would be the night of the most disastrous floods in East Anglia, in living memory.

Alan R. Carter was a young police officer at the time and that day was working the 2 till 10 shift. " . . . I remember during the early evening, possibly around 6 pm, standing on Pier Terrace when a massive hoarding attached to the wall outside the Palace Cinema was wrenched from its fittings by the tremendous winds. The hoarding was about thirty feet long and fifteen feet high and was used to advertise current and forthcoming attractions at the cinema. It tumbled across the road and finished up near the sweet shop, the nearest shop to the harbour. Luckily no-one was hit by it though I remember it was pretty close to a corporation bus which was passing at the time."

A man living in Walberswick had a telephone call from his father in Scarborough, warning him that a big tide had hit that part of the coast. However, sufficient warnings were not given and most people were unprepared and felt that they should have been alerted to the danger.

Mr Arthur Gibbs still owns the same shop in Whapload Road that he was running in 1953. " . . . My wife had just finished scrubbing the floor when Frank Swan, a lifeboatman, banged on our door and asked us if we were aware of what was happening. He told us that the sea was coming. When I looked, the lamp-post that used to be opposite the shop had water lapping round it. Within ten minutes the water was in the door, the windows were pushed out and the waves were smashing through the house . . .." The flood had begun.

Mrs Edna Wright who lived opposite, on the sea side of Whapload Road, was also alerted by Frank Swan, ". . . When I opened the front door to speak to him the water came over the step . . . Our cottage was a bit low and therefore the water seemed to reach us first . . .."

Mrs J. Mitchell of Bourne Road recalls, "My husband and I lived in a small cottage with my widowed mother and brother. It was situated on the corner of Wildes Street and East Street in the Beach Village of Lowestoft. About 9.30 on that fateful night a young policeman knocked on the door to tell us of possible flooding. As he was telling us the water was swirling about his feet and he said a few words like, 'Bloody hell it's here!' and then took to his heels and ran. We put two armchairs on top of the table and that's all we had time to do before the water came rushing in. My husband, brother and I ran upstairs, my mother was round my aunt's."

Alan Carter was by now on duty at the police station and took a telephone call to the effect that water was pouring into the basement at Barclays Bank which stood on the corner of Commercial Road and London Road South. ". . . I believe that this was the first report of flooding in Lowestoft that night though they came in thick and fast after then . . .."

A twenty-six foot high tide, the highest ever recorded, split Lowestoft and Oulton Broad in two. The sea had invaded the town, reaching such places as the engine room at the Norwich Road electricity works while on the south side of the bridge, Belvedere Road and St. John's Road were quickly flooded. The worst affected area though was the Beach Village, where the low-lying streets were soon waist deep, with the water level on the pickling plots and the net drying ground soon rising to four or five feet.

Whapload Road, barely recognisable here as the industrial area it is today, was one of the first areas of the town to be flooded.

The old Eagle Brewery on Whapload Road was one of many premises that suffered damage as a result of the flooding. When this building was demolished one of the ornamental eagles was unfortunately broken, although the other one is now sited by the main entrance to the office at Birds Eye Wall's Ltd.

Jack Guymer was another policeman who was on duty that night. ". . . We'd had our tea and Nobby Clark told me to go down to the beach and see what the situation was. I went down north of the Gas Works and I saw across the Denes this great big wall of white water and I ran round as many houses as I could saying, 'Tell your neighbours, there's going to be a flood!' And I ran back to the police station and Superintendent Clarke said to me, 'How much do you think the damage will come to?' It was an impossible question."

Mr Gus Jensen, the then licensee of the *Rising Sun* in Lowestoft's Beach Village, remembers, ". . . I was in the bar that night. People began to say there was water coming up. Some of my customers got away but those who hung on to the last minute got their feet wet! Dot, my wife and my baby daughter went upstairs, and my grandfather held the fort at the door, while I went to see what I could do. I started at 11 o'clock and I was in the water till 6.30 the following morning . . .."

With other men of the village Mr Jensen also made a round of all the houses, warning the occupants. Many of the villagers had experience of past flooding and had already begun to fix floodboards to their doors which were to prove hopelessly ineffective in the face of the torrent which swept through the streets within a matter of minutes.

One family in East Street first knew something was wrong when there was a loud knocking on the door and a man told them to put floodboards up. Mr E. A. J. Hill, now of Oulton Broad, was fifteen years old and after moving from London had lived in the Beach Village with his family for four years. ". . . My father turned to my mother and said, 'What the hell are floodboards and what do you do with them?' We were not used to hearing about floods like the people who were brought up in the area . . . We all looked out of the window and saw water coming down the street . . . We grabbed what we could and went upstairs to the bedroom . . .."

One man who lived in Maltsters Score barricaded his front door and then opened the back door to see where the water was and let it all in!

The bar of the *Gas House Tavern*, a public house in the Beach area, was crowded that night. The licensee, Fred Brady remembered, "It was about 10 minutes to 10 when a chap suddenly stuck his head round the door and shouted for everyone to get home. I have never seen a bar clear so quickly in all my life . . .."

In addition to damaging property, the flooding also caused the deaths of numerous domestic animals. Inspector Frank Woods of the R.S.P.C.A. pictured here, estimated that between thirty and forty pigs were drowned in the Whapload Road area. Woods worked from dawn till after dark on that Sunday and rescued more than thirty animals, amongst them cats, dogs, chickens, pigs, budgerigars and rabbits. Many of these animals were kept at the R.S.P.C.A. headquarters until they could be returned home.

Gasworks Road in the Beach Village. The Gas Works was flooded to an average depth of three feet with many people losing their gas supply for a week as a result. The Navy toured the Beach to see if any residents required assistance.

It was just before 10 o'clock on that Saturday night when the sea rushed into the low-lying streets of the Beach Village. By the next morning you still needed a dinghy to get round the Anguish Street area.

Amongst the crowds leaving the *Gas House Tavern* was Mrs F. Tuck and her husband, who lived in Wildes Street. "... At about 10 o'clock the police came in and said, 'Get home at once, there's a flood warning!' We were home in five minutes and by then water was coming in both back and front doors. We didn't have much time to save anything apart from putting the settee up on a table before we had to get upstairs. Soon the water was up six stairs and we were marooned all night with my two girls and a friend. It was so cold! I had a roll of wallpaper in the cupboard so I burnt it in the fireplace to try to get warm ...."

The Rev. P. Street was the Vicar of Christchurch in Whapload Road and he was having a bath at the Vicarage when the phone rang. "It was around 10.30. I answered the phone and it was the police with disturbing news. 'Your Church is under water!' they told me, 'You'd better come quick!' I made a hasty finish to my bath and arrived at the Church shortly before 11 to find that the Church was indeed under water. The lady in the small shop opposite told me later that she knew there must be something wrong because when she looked out of the window she saw a policeman swimming into the front door of the Church ...."

Mr F. E. Goode of Allen Road, Oulton Broad, was travelling on the last train from London and was held up at Beccles Station only to be told that Lowestoft Station was up to platform level with water. He continues, "... At 9.30 we were waiting to hear if we could proceed. After a while the train moved off very slowly as much of the track was under water. Arriving at Oulton Broad South Station we were told that the train was going no further. The passengers for Lowestoft made their own way home while the train and coaches were put in the sidings for the night ...."

Mr W. Solomon, Assistant Harbour Master at Oulton Broad, was securing boats at the Yacht Club for about an hour before the actual flooding. "I knew we were going to have a high tide," he said, "and I was anxious to get everything secure. I had just finished at about 9.30 and was walking up the quay towards Waller's Restaurant when I saw a wall of water coming through towards me ...."

The water had surged up the inner harbour to Oulton Broad, where it tore a sixteen-foot gap in an earthen retaining wall and poured into the rear of Waller's Restaurant and Shop. Mr Solomon continues, "... The torrent divided in two. One arm went

Bridge Road, Oulton Broad. A local man surveys the extent of the damage to the road, which was undermined by the water.

Some idea of the water level in Everitt's Park can be judged from the railings and the bandstand which is shown standing in the middle of the flood. This area became a continuation of the sea.

round the Lake Lothing side of Waller's and the other arm between the Restaurant and the *Lady of the Lake* public-house. It was coming through both places in an avalanche and the *Lady of the Lake* was about six feet deep in water." It swept across the main road, inundating Nicholas Everitt Park, smashing the quays at the Yacht Station with the small boats hurled ashore.

By this time the flood had reached towns and villages further down the coast. Mrs G. M. Meekin, now of Colchester, was living at Walberswick with her husband and four children. ". . . My husband had been to the *Anchor Hotel* to play darts and when he came home during the evening he said the water was up to the telephone box on the edge of the green! Although we lived on the green, we were luckily on a hill, otherwise we would have had the water in our home . . .."

Others were not so fortunate. "We got flooded first because our cottage in East Street went down into a dip," remembers one Lowestoft resident, "We'd been to a party and we came home about 9.30 and we got a beautiful fire built up in our little cottage. We decided to pull our mats up and try to put as much as we could on top of the sideboard, but we put too much on it and it tipped over!"

Rosemary Moffat now of Uggleshall, Beccles was living in London Road South and looking forward to her eighth birthday on the 3rd February. She recalls, ". . . The sea came in at the front and the river at the back. My Dad put a mattress against the front door in a hopeless attempt to keep the water out but in the end we had to move upstairs to the bedroom. The two most vivid memories I have are the high-pitched screaming wind which I can still hear, and the Cadburys Mini Rolls in silver paper which were supposed to be for my birthday party. We had a whole tin of them and my Mum, Dad and I ate the lot."

Peter Hemsley lived at 53 London Road South with his wife Connie and his mother and father. He remembers, ". . . I went up to have a bath while my wife was getting supper ready and all at once the doorbell went and someone said, 'Have you seen in your garden? All the water's coming up!' I came down and we shut all the doors and the water started to rise. The thing I remember is the water coming up on the outside of our front bay window. It was like looking into a goldfish bowl! . . . We got upstairs

Looking up London Road South, near where Peter Hemsley lived with his wife and parents. He says he will always remember a policeman swimming past his house, complete with helmet!

with my parents, we had a good fire as we had the flat above. Then Johnnie May who lived next door put his head out of the window and shouted, 'Fancy a dip, Peter!'" He adds, ". . . I will always remember a policeman swimming past the house. Complete with helmet . . .."

Mrs Floyd lived in the middle one of three houses next to the bowling green near Sparrow's Nest. Actual waves crashed through her front door and reached as high as eight or nine stairs! She remembers, ". . . The child's high chair drifted out of the broken window, and floated away!"

Jimmy Grimmer lived at 283 Whapload Road. ". . . By 10.30 it was coming into the front room and reached as high as the top of the fireplace, about four foot six . . .."

Next door Mr Gibbs and his wife had managed to get upstairs, taking with them a family who lived opposite. They had tried to escape from the flood but were stopped by the waves which knocked over their little boy. Mr Gibbs recalls, ". . . Luckily we had plenty of coal. We kept it in every room. We had enough of the stuff to keep us warm all night. Their baby was coughing and spluttering with what turned out to be pneumonia, so we got a drawer and tried to make it comfortable in there. Then the father, the grandfather and I tried to go downstairs but there were fish boxes and all kinds of rubbish swirling about in the current. In ten minutes the staircase was chock-a-block with rubbish. Luckily we got back upstairs before the sea knocked the front door off and smashed a showcase right behind our heels. We kept the fire going all night, keeping the kiddy as warm as we could."

Edna Wright who lived at Marsh Cottage continues, ". . . My husband took one of the boys up the slope to safety and came back for the other one saying he'd come back for me and our girl. I said, 'I'm not stopping here!' as the water was rising quickly, so I picked up my little girl and said, 'Now you cling to mam and I don't care if you pull my hair out, I'll get you up there.' We managed to scramble to safety . . .'

Doris E. James kept the *Kumfy Kafe* with her husband, Ron. Both of them and their two children, Carole and Ronnie, were in bed with 'flu' but it was Mrs James who awoke to a loud banging on the front door. "The wind was howling, it was a noisy night. I went downstairs and could hear loud voices, but couldn't understand what they were saying so opened the door. The water rushed in eighteen inches deep right up the

The Oval and the hockey pitch were completely submerged, with the salt water doing considerable damage to the turf. It can be seen from the trees that the wind was still blowing from the north even by the following morning.

At the rear of the Gas Works was the *Kumfy Kafe* which was run by Mrs James and her husband. This picture shows a man rolling away a herring barrel, one of the many that were strewn around the area by the previous night's torrents of water.

hallway!'' Mrs James couldn't shut the door as there was too much water, so hurried back upstairs and as she did the lights went out. ''. . . I could hear the water rushing through the house. We kept the *Kumfy Kafe* but it wasn't very 'kumfy' that night. I kept counting the stairs to see how many were left before my feet touched the water. I could hear our cat meowing on the roof which upset the children so I got out onto the top windowsill and somehow managed to get the poor bedraggled animal off the roof . . .''

She continues, ''. . . The huge logs on the green opposite, were tossed about like matchsticks, they piled up at the side of the house in East Street, smashed the front door of the café and overturned the counters.''

The logs, many of them forty feet long and two feet thick, had been stacked on the pickling plots and were a great menace that night. Mr Hill remembers, ''. . . As the water started to get deeper so the logs started to move. The only way they could go was down East Street past our cottage. At the time my parents were very calm and didn't look upon this as the disaster it was. As we looked out of the window we saw the logs come floating down the road. We started to bet with each other as to which one was going to come through the window first. Luckily for us none of them did . . .''

Swirling with the logs in the strong current was debris such as barrels of herring, fish boxes, huge wooden piles and pieces of furniture. At the rear of Rant Score East there was also a load of very large tree trunks.

As Mr Jensen made his way round the Beach Village warning people of the flood, he suddenly remembered his fourteen pigs. ''. . . I had just got them out and was herding them along when I looked up East Street. The water was rising rapidly and all at once I saw a mass of tree trunks tearing down at me. They were coming down at a terrific rate and were filling the entire road from side to side. I remember thinking, 'This is it, you've had it.' I didn't expect to live. I had one pig under my arm and I kept hold of it and just closed my eyes and waited. I still don't see how all the logs missed me and carried on swirling down the street bashing into houses and walls.''

Tuttle's horse was also in danger that night. The department store kept the animal in stables on Whapload Road but fortunately it was pulled to safety. Mr Alexander, who lived in Mariner Street at the time, remembers, ''. . . My father was working at the gasworks on the 2 to 10 shift and when the flood happened he came home and told my uncle, George Coles and his boy who looked after the horse. They got it out of its stable and up the bank . . ..

By 10 o'clock the 'wall of water' had completely engulfed the Beach Village. A few people had managed to leave the area before the worst of the flood but the majority were cut off by the rising water and forced back into their homes and up their stairs. In all nearly four hundred houses were flooded in addition to the business premises in the centre of the town and the Beach Village, as the waves swept in over the new £300,000 sea wall. Throughout the night Mr Jensen along with Billy Boothroyd and Dan Dyer kept up their constant patrol, waist deep in water. "It was a terrific current," recalled Mr Jensen, "just outside Christchurch seemed to be the worst. I was waist deep in water there and the current kept shooting my feet off the ground."

In her small cottage on the corner of Wildes Street the situation was worsening for Mrs Mitchell. ". . . Some of the logs that were sailing down East Street were hitting out cottage and making it tremble. Our staircase was closed off by a wooden door and when the water had reached the fifth stair my husband went down to see if there was any way we could get out. As he forced the staircase door open there was an almighty bang and a blue flash as the electric meter blew up. My husband returned back upstairs and the three of us sat on the bed, very frightened . . .."

This picture shows East Street where some of the logs came to rest. The logs, many of them forty feet long and two feet thick, had been stacked near the pickling plots before the sea swept them like matchsticks through the Village. Miraculously they did no serious damage, although the torrent pounded and battered them against the walls of many homes in the area.

Throughout that Saturday night, Coastguard Mr R. S. Cooper and his son Ronald were marooned in the look-out on Ness Point. As the storm raged before them, huge waves swept over the sea wall and pounded the small wooden hut, which was one of the few buildings left standing in the sea wall vicinity. "I must say I felt a little nervous during the storm when the old look-out was shaking and trembling," admitted Coastguard Cooper, "but they really built these look-outs and I shall never be nervous of staying out on watch again, whatever the weather!" At 3 am fellow Coastguard Mr E. Burbidge somehow managed to get to the wooden hut though not to rescue the occupants but to relieve Mr Cooper at his post!

Hamilton Road, where sight-seeing locals check the damage. The railway line has almost disappeared under a pile of debris. The barrels of herring weighed around a ton and were thrown around by the swirling water with horrifying ease. When some people returned to their properties, they found the barrels had smashed through their windows and ended up in their front rooms!

In spite of the buffeting by waves all Saturday night, the newly-built Claremont Pier Pavilion, which was experiencing its first severe storm, suffered little damage except for broken windows.

SECTION 2

"We Got Trouble"

"I noticed that the sea was getting extremely rough," remembers Mr A. J. Willimot now of Oulton Broad, "worse than I had ever seen it before." Mr Willimot was sitting in the lounge bar at the Claremont Pier, and enjoying a Saturday night out. He recalls, ". . . the rough sea didn't worry me at first, until the waves started to smash the windows and the water began to crash over the ramp at the side of the pier . . .."

It happened so quickly. The sea swept over the quays at Trawl Dock and poured rapidly into the streets all round the Central Railway Station. Soon it became like a river, surging round Tuttle's corner . . .."

London Road was flooded as far as Beach Road, with water covering Denmark Road and Bevan Street, pouring across from the fish markets. Another man remembers, "I lived in Bevan Street and that got flooded along with Tonning Street, where Jim Carver had a little café. He used to go round with a bell, selling rolls. He was flooded. It didn't go as far as Raglan Street though."

In London Road South, in the Windsor Road area, the water was said to have been several feet higher than at St. John's Church. One man's rabbits were even drowned in their hutches in Beaconsfield Road with the flood reaching up Carlton Road as far as the *Fighting Cocks* public house. Mr Bagshaw was then a taxi driver and each night had to take a regular customer to Carlton Road from the Crown Hotel. ". . . I couldn't get through the flood so I had to take him via St. Olaves but I could only charge him the usual fare of half-a-crown!"

This photograph was taken from the **Horn Hill Railway Bridge** and shows the flooded railway line which used to run from the docks to Oulton Broad South via Kirkley Ham and Victoria Road.

Soon the alarm was raised that Lowestoft was being flooded and the emergency services were called into action. As the first reports of the flooding arrived at the Normanston Fire Service Headquarters, Divisional Officer Ron Bishop, who was at a party in Hopton, was contacted and told of the situation. ". . . I decided to go, apologised to my wife and the host and said I'd be back in half an hour. I went back to the station where all hell had broken loose." He immediately mobilised all the men at his disposal, including the retained firemen and members of the Auxiliary Fire Service. He divided Lowestoft into sections and sent an appliance with an officer in charge to each with instructions to do what they could. It was impossible to begin pumping-out operations straight away though, as Ron Bishop explains, ". . . You can't pump out till the water level drops. If you've got a building with water up to the bedroom windows and start pumping it out, the pressure from inside will collapse the building. You've got to be patient, wait till the water goes down outside, then you can pump out what's inside . . .."

However, the seventy men of the Fire Service were important members of the rescue work that night. Leading Fireman Frederick Barlow was in the area of St. John's Road, where the water was over five feet deep in places. People at upstairs windows drew his attention to an object in the water further up the street.

Fred Barlow explained, "I thought at first it was a dog, but when I got closer I could see it was a man. He seemed to be in the later stages of exhaustion and as I reached him he disappeared under the water. By that time the water was up to my neck but I managed to grab him and struggle down the street." With the help of Fireman J. Roach, the half-drowned man was taken into the comfort of a nearby house where a lady fetched blankets and did all she could for him. Mr Barlow continued, "The man was unconscious and we applied artificial respiration until the arrival of the ambulance." Having saved the man's life the two firemen returned to work, remaining on duty for a further four hours.

Meanwhile, Ron Bishop rang Superintendent Clarke of the police, ". . . I said, 'We got trouble.' He said, 'It looks like it,' so we decided to meet at the fire station along with the Town Clerk and the Mayor. So they could co-ordinate the operation, we agreed that all the emergency calls should be put through the police station. The Town Clerk,

St. John's Road at the rear of Mann Egertons Ltd, where water was over five feet deep in places during that night and was the scene of a daring rescue by two firemen of a man who was close to drowning. By the morning after there was still plenty of water as this picture shows, and a life raft can be seen on the left of the picture.

the Mayor and I drove round the area, it was all pretty hectic. I was involved in the St. John's Church rescue too. I didn't get to my bed that night . . .."

The full effect of the flood was still dawning on many people though. As a young girl of fifteen, Margaret Howell née Bemment had just returned from Beccles on the train and at Oulton Broad South Station was told to disembark as Oulton Broad and Lowestoft were flooded. ". . . On arriving at Waller's Shop and seeing the water I began to wonder if I should ever get home that night. After standing there for about an hour a car driver made an attempt at crossing the bridge and said he would take two passengers. I was lucky enough to be one of them. Needless to say on reaching the brow of the bridge the car broke down, but we managed to get a lift from a taxi driver returning to Lowestoft."

Mr F. E. Goode of Allen Road, Oulton Broad was aboard the same train, travelling home from London. As he began to make his way home from the station he found, ". . . At the Victoria Road and Bridge Road junction I could see lights and lots of people outside Waller's Restaurant as far as the foot of the bridge. I found the water on the salt side so high that it had broken over the bank and was well above the level of the lock gates. Two men in thigh boots were taking people, rich and poor, back across the water. I could do nothing other than go home."

Gordon Steward was a police officer with the British Transport Police who had an office outside Lowestoft's Railway Station. He left his Carlton Colville home at 9.30 that evening to go to work. He remembers, ". . . I went Oulton Broad way on my pushbike. When I got to Waller's the water was pouring out of the windows. It was impossible to get past and the only way I could get to work was to go up Victoria Road, to the line gates and walk down the line to Harbour Road. I asked permission to do this by ringing up at the line gate house there. I went back and got all the people who wanted to go across. I felt like the Pied Piper with twenty or thirty people following me down Victoria Road, down the line and across the railway bridge into Harbour Road . . .."

Mr Claud Hamilton lived with his wife on the wherry *Claudian* which that night was moored securely at the Broads end of Lake Lothing. Mr Hamilton only had one leg and was well-known all over the Broads as 'Long John Silver'. He recalled, ". . . My

The Oulton Broad Railway Bridge, officially called the Carlton Swing Bridge, proved the only means home for many people that night. There were no trains to worry about as the line was washed away between Beccles and Lowestoft, and many people walked across it. Among them was Gordon Steward, a police officer with the British Transport Police, who, after receiving permission, led twenty or thirty people across the bridge and ". . . felt like the Pied Piper!"

Home of Mr Hamilton, the wherry *Claudian* was swept over a derelict drifter during the flood and was left stranded there when the water subsided.

wife had just poured two cups of tea when I went up for a final check-up. As soon as I stuck my head out of the hatch I realised that things had started to happen. The wherry had swung round. The position was serious because of the wrecks in the vicinity. With the height of the water these hulks, which normally stand eight or ten feet out of the water, had almost completely disappeared leaving only a few stumps showing. I was afraid we might drift over the top of one of these wrecks and then, when the tide fell, the wherry would turn over . . ..''

The only thing Mr Hamilton could do was cut the stern rope, in the hope of drifting onto a mud bank. He continues, ''. . . I cut the wherry adrift and the tide started to carry us between two stumps which later turned out to be two drifters. Just as I thought we were going to drift clear, we stuck, and there was nothing I could do to shift her . . ..'' Mr Hamilton, fearing for the safety of his wife, grabbed his gun and began firing shots into the air, which attracted the attention of Mr Russell Bessey who effected a rescue.

Mr Catchpole was also in Oulton Broad, ''. . . We were having the Scouts' Christmas Party at St. Mark's Church, Oulton Broad and the lights went out and we eventually realised that it was flooded and went down to the park. We came back because no-one could get home and I rang up my Mum, so my Mum had everybody sleeping at hers, about five or six . . . When we got home, my brother hadn't realised what had happened and had kept putting coins in the meter, thinking that it had run out!''

At Pakefield Mr Pickess remembers seeing the sea smashing into the chalets along the front. Soon they were just broken bits of wood, the sea scooping up the pieces in its swell and smashing them again and again against the parapet until the remnants of the chalets were completely destroyed. Meanwhile at Kessingland, the front half of the lifeboat shed was washed away!

Southwold and its surrounding area was devastated by the destructive surge of the North Sea. Mrs Meeking remembers, ''. . . My husband and Arthur Sharman were out all night rescuing people from bedroom windows. It was a terrible night and there were people drowned in the houses along Ferry Road on the Southwold side. I did hear that the ambulance was called out there and was turned over by a wave. Two men who were in it were washed out and landed on Southwold Common and were found next morning,

The Bridge Road area of Oulton Broad was one of many places where the flooding caused large holes to appear in the undermined road. This left large chunks of concrete beneath the water and with manhole covers also displaced any car that attempted to drive through the flooding did so at great risk.

At Oulton Broad the Yacht Station was wrecked and boats were sunk while trees were pushed over by the force of the water. The chair on the left of the photograph is from Waller's Restaurant.

still alive! It was a miracle.''

What had begun as a Saturday night out for many was fast turning into a nightmare. ''. . . During that evening stories started to filter through of quite severe flooding at or near the bridge, together with the news that Oulton Broad was cut off,'' recalls Mr Tony Hooks of Worlingham who was at the time courting his wife at the Palais de Danse in Pakefield. ''It all seemed so unreal although I began to have slight doubts about how I could get home back over the bridge.''

However, even though the lights went out at the Palais, the dancing didn't stop! Mr Hook explains, ''. . . One of the main exit doors was opened and an enterprising individual drove a car partially into the dance hall and switched his lights on full. For some ten minutes the band continued playing while we danced to those single car lights.''

Mr Hook still had to get home to Tennyson Road though. ''. . . We left soon after and I recall cycling home with some trepidation as I approached the bridge. The southern approaches were fine but as soon as I got over the bridge, I found Tuttles and Station Square were badly flooded. I hoisted up my trousers and pedalled like mad through the water whilst onlookers cheered me across. Apart from a good soaking I got through all right, totally unaware of the serious situation elsewhere . . ..''

There was also a dance at the Victoria Hotel in London Road South. Many of the guests thought it was a prank when the lights suddenly went out until it was announced that the whole of the centre of the town was flooded and anyone needing to sleep on the floor could do so. One of the crowd decided to try to make it home, only getting as far as where Mann Egerton's is today, though with Oulton Broad flooded too, many people found themselves stranded that night.

At the Suffolk Hotel the annual dinner of the Lowestoft Choral Society was being held, attended by about one hundred and twenty members and friends. As soon as the hotel's manager, Mr Charles A. Smith, realised that there was about a foot of water in the street, he warned his guests of the situation. Several car-owners left to get their vehicles to safety but the majority of the guests were unperturbed, and continued with their party, unaware of the extent of the flooding. Mr Smith found Bert the barman in the public bar, sweeping the water back with a broom, ''. . . I told him to take a look outside the door. When he opened it, the water rushed in!''

Mr Smith's naval training alerted him to the potential danger in the cellars which contained boilers, electric mains and the stores of food, fuel and liquor, an explosive cocktail. By wading waist deep in the water to pull the electric fuses and draw the boilers, Mr Smith averted a possible explosion. Then he rushed back upstairs to entertain the guests who had been joined by the people from the public-bar. It was certainly a busy night for the hotel manager!

Mr Smith continued, ''. . . the most frightening thing was that as the water rose in the cellar, the compressed air which was forced out made the building rock. My children were terrified.''

Mrs Anne Day, steward of the Yacht Club remembers, ''. . . We went down in the cellar that night not realising that the other side of the nine inch wall was solid water. The boiler room was completely flooded. It was only when the fireman came up and said, 'The wall could go any minute,' that we realised. In the end it did flood, it seeped through a couple of bricks. My daughter, Penny, was so distressed because her favourite doll she called Miranda had been left in the cellar and was washed away . . ..''

Though policeman Jack Guymer was on duty, he was able to rescue his wife who was at the Choral Society's dinner. ''. . . By the time I got there the water was about a foot deep. So I piggy-backed her out and some of the ladies there thought I was going to piggy-back the lot of them!''

Some of them did get piggy-backs though. Bridget Patrick's mother was one of the ladies carried over the bridge after attending the dinner that evening. She arrived home at four o'clock in the morning!

Elsewhere in the town other functions were being interrupted. At St. Margaret's Institute there was a table tennis championship being held. The competitors came from as far afield as Stowmarket, Ipswich and Bury but couldn't get home because of the flooding. Fortunately, the headmaster of the Briar Clyffe School, Mr Levine, came to the rescue and allowed them to stay the night at the school.

Lowestoft Town F.C. were returning from an away match at King's Lynn. It took a long time to get back to the town as there were so many detours and even when they were back in the town, the bus had to wait a long time in the Carlton Road area and then had to drive through quite deep water.

At the Royal Hotel a dinner and dance for the St. John's Ambulance Service was being held. When the lights suddenly went out, Brian Poppy, a member of the service, remembers, ". . . Candles were lit and then somebody said, 'Quick! Look out of the window!' And then we realised the sea was right up to the doors. It didn't take long for the service to spring into action to help those who needed it." Mr Stanley Balls, a volunteer driver, remembers, ". . . In those days one of the ambulances was an old Army one, which was high enough to drive over the bridge through the flood. The service also had a car which we used through the night to carry people about."

Brian Poppy couldn't get over the bridge until 3 am, and even then it was in the St. John's Ambulance. ". . . We had a flat in Denmark Road which was flooded so we were driven up to my mother-in-law's house in Edinburgh Road. My wife stayed the night there, but I borrowed my father-in-law's rubber boots, and then went back to the ambulance depot to see what I could do."

Mrs Violet Watling, now aged ninety-two, recalls how her brother Gordon Stebbings was an active member of the St. John's Ambulance Service and spent the night working with his colleagues rescuing people from the St. John's Church area.

Stanley Armes was at the *Marquis of Lorne* and remembers, ". . . My younger brother was at the Palace Cinema with his girlfriend who lived in Kirkley. He walked her home and came and told me that I wouldn't be able to get over the bridge because of the flooding. At home in Ipswich Road my mother knew nothing about it, she could cook on her gas cooker, she wasn't affected at all. Of course, she wondered where we had got to! We weren't allowed out late so when we turned up next day, having stayed the night at friends', we were the first to tell her about what had happened."

Mr Steward, a transport policeman, got through the flood that night to get to work, an office outside the railway station. He recalls, ". . . I couldn't put on my uniform as it had got wet in my locker so I kept my RAF flying jacket on and helmet and waded into the water. It was awful weather, wind, sleet, the lot. I got to the railway station refreshment rooms where there were some old ladies who couldn't get out. So I went to the harbour yards where my father was a night watchman, borrowed a pair of thigh boots and a wheel barrow and went back to the refreshment rooms. I got the three or

The Royal Hotel Ballroom, pictured on the right, where the dinner and dance for the St. John's Ambulance Service took place that night. Note the battered slope down to the beach and the broken groynes, indications of the force of the waves.

four ladies to sit in the barrow and pushed them down Rotterdam Road to the two pubs near Trafalgar Street. Then I helped some people standing on Driscoll's Corner . . . When I went across to the trawl dock I was surprised to see the bows of the boats were on the top of the quay. Some of the ships' husbands were there and we started to rock these boats back and forward to slide them back in the water . . .''

"I finished my beer in the bar of the Suffolk Hotel, stepped out of the door and there was water up to the top step and everywhere in front of me, right across to Tuttles,'' remembers one man. "The lights were still on in the shop although the water was now two feet deep! I was stuck in the pub till three o-clock Sunday morning . . . When the water went down to eighteen inches some of the fish market chaps in their thigh boots were charging half-a-crown to piggy-back people across to Driscoll's Corner at the bottom of Commercial Road.''

June Gotts was supposed to be celebrating her twenty-second birthday that evening though the party had to be cancelled! She recalls, "I walked to my friend's in Seago Street and was almost hit by a falling chimney stack. My friend said it could have been worse!'' However, the thing she remembers most about that night was what haunted many people — the noise that was coming from the turbulent sea that was driving over the Denes.

Junction of London Road South and Belvedere Road, with the Palace Cinema in the centre. The cinema was showing *Singin' in the Rain* that fateful night. There was a tremendous amount of debris left by the flood and shown here amongst the rubbish are some of the railway sleepers that had broken adrift from the storage yard on the other side of the river.

SECTION 3

"Singin' in the Rain"

One of the most popular venues that evening was the Palace Cinema which was situated near the bridge in premises which until recently were occupied by Notley's Estate Agents. Ironically, it was showing *Singing' in the Rain* though few could have realised that many would see real-life drama that night, more memorable than any film could ever be.

Bob Pye of Higher Driver, Lowestoft, was at the Palace that night, with his girlfriend, now his wife. They were originally going to the Odeon Cinema but because of the strong wind decided to go to the Palace instead. The first Mr Pye knew about the flood was when, "... People in the front seats started moving towards the back saying their feet were getting wet!" A Mrs Cowlbeck remembers that she didn't think the noise she could hear was water gushing in, she just thought that the film's sound effects were good! Eventually the cinema's manager came to the front and said that he was going to stop the film as the tide was very high and overflowing on to the quay. Mr Pye remembers that after leaving through the back of the cinema, "... We went and had a look and saw the water was lapping the bridge!"

A few of the cinema-goers didn't make it across the bridge so returned to the Palace and sat in the coffee bar. By this time there was no electricity so they had to sit in candlelight.

Leon Harvey was another at the cinema that evening. ".... On leaving and reaching the Palace entrance by the foyer I saw a small rowing dinghy making its way across the flooded roads to rescue some people who were trapped inside St. John's Church. I then walked from the cinema to the market which in those days was always accessible and saw the fishing boats riding high in the dock with water several inches above the quayside."

Mr Harvey made his way home to Waveney Crescent via Marine Parade and Horn Hill as the lower end of London Road South was flooded. ". . . I found that flood water was racing across the road at the point where Richards' lower yard and the Co-op met. Not wishing to get wet and being a very clever seventeen-year-old, I decided to tightrope walk Richards' old rounded metal fence and keep dry! I got about half way across and lost my balance, falling into the water up to my waist on Richards' side. Luckily I managed to scramble out rather wet and cold and made my way back home. At that time the water was on Waveney Drive just beyond the Post Office box at the junction of Durban Road. I wasn't exactly 'singin' in the rain' that night but just regretted getting so wet and cold that night so long ago!"

Jimmy Grimmer had just left school in 1953 and started at the Coachworks. It was a little after 10 when he and his mate left the Palace Cinema, although they managed to get a bus over the bridge. ". . . I lived in Whapload Road with my parents and as I came down Mariners Score the water had started to lap the road . . .."

At least two buses made it over the bridge in high water that night. Mr C. E. Dalley of Carlton Colville, was an Eastern Counties bus conductor and he remembers first reaching the bridge about 10 o'clock on a bus returning from Kessingland. ". . . It couldn't get over because of the water and so swung round in Middle Drive and went back to Kessingland, picking up passengers along the way. By the time the bus reached Kessingland it wasn't able to get down by the beach and so headed back to Lowestoft, turning round half-way up Church Road at about 10.25."

At around 10.40 the bus arrived back at the Palace Cinema, where the water was now covering the bridge. Mr Dalley continues, ". . . The driver of the bus, Cyril Bunn, turned to me and said, 'What are we going to do?' There were loads of people on the bus, all of whom wanted to get over the bridge. So Bunn said, 'Get up the bloody stairs, I'm going through!' He put the bus into second gear and it made its way slowly over the bridge and just kept going . . .." The forward thrust of the bus caused the water to be pushed right up to the driver's seat in the cab but he kept his foot hard on the

Two buses make their way through the water near the Palace Cinema, though whether these were the buses that made it across the bridge that night is unknown.

throttle and made it across. ". . . The bus couldn't get through Station Square as in those days there was a dip there, so it went down Waveney Road instead . . . The windows of Tuttles were all out and wardrobes and all kinds of furniture were drifting out of the store! . . .."

Bob Pye also recalls the bus diverting up Waveney Road and into Beach Road and then up the High Street and saw a car at the traffic lights near Tuttles with water halfway up its body.

The bus returned to the station at about 10.50 and Mr Dalley and Cyril Bunn were about to go home, expecting that the 10.50 service to Kessingland would be cancelled, when the bus inspector ran out to meet them. "Get back on that bus," he shouted, "You're doing the 10 to 11!" The two men just kept walking though, "If this bugger's doing the 10 to 11," retorted Cyril Bunn, "you ought to get up in the cab yourself!"

Another couple who took a bus over the bridge that night were Mr and Mrs Cleveland, now of Norfolk Street. They had also been to the Palace Cinema but were not yet aware of the enormity of the flooding. It was only when Mrs Cleveland looked out of the window of her High Street home, that she realised that the sea was breaking over the sea wall. ". . . The noise was like an express train. The next thing there were screams coming from down Whapload Road . . .."

Mr Willimot, who had been spending a quiet night at the Claremont Pier, was another who came across the bridge on a bus. He recalls, ". . . Where I lived at Surrey Street and outside the General Post Office the water was about a foot deep. Luckily we were living in a flat above the fifty-shilling tailors shop but I could see my wife looking out of the window with a horrified expression on her face. She was from Berlin and had never seen anything like this before. Come to think of it, neither had I!"

Mr Dalley, the conductor on one of the last buses over the bridge, even had a hazardous bicycle ride home to Carlton Colville that night, ". . . A group of us left work together and we rode down Clapham Road. We just managed to spot in time that the force of the water had pushed the cellar doors open, otherwise someone could have been in for a nasty dive . . .." The group tried to avoid the flooding, but in the end decided to wade through it. Mr Dalley recalls, ". . . There wasn't much water on the bridge by this time, though on the approaches the water reached waist high!"

London Road North, taken from near the General Post Office looking towards Tuttle's corner. On the extreme right hand side of the photograph is one of the buses that managed to cross the bridge but had to divert into Waveney Road as the water was too deep in Station Square.

Police officer Alan Carter was due off duty at 10 o'clock but in the circumstances had no choice but to stay and help. He was sent to a house in Denmark Road to investigate reports that a woman was screaming for help, ". . . I could hear the woman still screaming and as she didn't answer my calls (she probably couldn't hear me) I entered the water and made towards her house. When it reached my waist I started to swim because I was aware that the flooding had caused drain covers to lift and I was terrified that I would plunge into an uncovered drain and be gone forever. I clearly remember thinking what a crazy way this was of earning a living — it was blowing a blizzard, extreme gale force winds, freezing cold water and here I was swimming along Denmark Road in the pitch darkness still wearing my policeman's helmet! . . .."

The house in which the lady was trapped was flooded only to a depth of about a foot. She was upstairs and quite safe so Mr Carter reassured her and made his way back. He decided that it would be easier if he went along Rotterdam Road instead of down Denmark Road and returned to the police station where he reported that the lady was safe. He went into the basement boiler room to get out of his wet clothing though all there was to wear was a rough denim boiler suit, ". . . Not very comfortable next to bare skin!" Mr Carter recalls.

By the time he went into the control room a panic had set in. ". . . A member of the public had telephoned to report that a policeman was believed drowned in Denmark Road. It transpired that the caller had seen an officer go into the water and almost an hour later he still hadn't returned. I realised they were talking about me and the caller was not aware that I had returned along a different road!"

"I was finally released from duty at 3 in the morning and instructed to report back at 8 for another tour — what a night!"

Another remarkable story took place in Oulton Broad where one old couple had a narrow escape. While the storm was at its peak they tried to make their way home to Carlton Colville but got cut off by the invading tide. Luckily the Assistant Harbour Master of Oulton Broad, Mr Solomon, was helping another young man across the bridge when he heard the old couple's faint cries for help. Looking around he saw the old folk sitting on top of a wall between two currents of water. They had been sitting there for half an hour having waded waist deep through the torrent before they decided

Concrete, iron railings, nothing seemed strong enough to bear the full force of the 'wall of water' at Oulton Broad.

Roaring through a sixteen-foot gap in the old river bank, a torrent of water burst in and around Waller's Shop and Restaurant at Oulton Broad. ''It was like an avalanche,'' said Mr Solomon, the Assistant Harbour Master.

The rear of Waller's Restaurant, Oulton Broad. Even the following morning the water was still pouring through the sixteen-foot gap in the retaining wall of Lake Lothing.

they could go no further. Mr Solomon and the young man carried them to safety, called for a taxi and then packed them off home.

Mr John Crisp worked for the Electricity Board and was called out at 11 o'clock to Southwold to try to make the electricity lines safe. He too was involved in a terrifying incident, ". . . As we went over the Southwold Bridge a wave smashed against our van and we ended up against a telegraph pole which is near to the bridge. Shaken up, we managed to get out of the van just in time. It was swept away . . .."

Swept off the road, John Crisp's van was still drifting in the flood water at Southwold the next morning.

However, some had no time to escape and five people in Southwold were killed. The victims all lived in Ferry Road and were three elderly women, whose bungalow disintegrated, and a thirty-nine-year-old woman and her four-year-old son. Indeed, that area of Southwold saw the worst of the destruction, the waves sweeping one Ferry Road bungalow several hundred yards out on the marshes which had become a vast lake. Finding themselves stranded the occupants, seven Americans including a young baby, could only clamber onto the roof and shout for help. Rowing boat crews were organised and car headlights lit up the scene, but initial attempts were unsuccessful due to the terrific winds and a snowstorm. Eventually however, through marvellous seamanship, former lifeboat coxswain Mobbs Mayhew and William Stannard managed to reach them and brought them safely to shore where they were put up by Mr and Mrs Jack Denny.

Southwold became an island with water up to four feet deep covering the only road out. The pier at the north end was badly damaged and beach huts were ripped away and smashed in the tumultuous waves. With Southwold cut off, many people were unable to get back into the town and spent an anxious night waiting for the water to recede.

The conditions that caused the flood also affected those out at sea. About eighty of the Lowestoft trawler fleet were at sea during the weekend and all weathered the storm without serious damage, with the sad exception of the motor trawler *Guava* which left port the day before the storm and was lost with all hands. The last that was heard of the vessel, one of the largest in the port and considered to be the safest, was a faint radio message picked up by another Lowestoft trawler on January 30th, ''I am hauling my gear and I am going to 'dodge'.'' One of the crew, Anthony Folkard, was just sixteen and taking part in his first voyage to sea. He took the place of Brian Isted who couldn't make the trip because of a broken wrist which he sustained on the vessel's previous journey. His father, Mr Dick Isted recalls, ''I remember saying that night, 'I'm glad my son's not out in that!' Little did I know that his ship was going down . . ..''

On January 30th, the day before the gale, the herring trawler *Guava* (LT73) set sail from Lowestoft. When she didn't return it was thought she must have extended her fishing trip to compensate for the days lost due to the bad weather. By the following Tuesday Mr D. A. Stephens, General Manager of Claridge Trawlers Ltd., announced, "After-consultation with the Naval authorities, I regret that all reasonable hope for them must be abandoned." Indeed, the *Guava* and her eleven man crew were never seen again.

Hamilton Dock, thirty-six hours after the flooding, with much of the debris remaining. The man walking back to his tanker is Jimmy Jacobs.

St. John's Church, the scene of the town's most famous rescue during the 1953 flood.

SECTION 4

The St. John's Church Rescue

Although there have been many accounts of the rescue at St. John's Church which took place that night, conflicting reports have resulted in the story becoming confused. The following has been reconstructed from information given by some of those involved in the rescue, and is as accurate as possible from the available facts.

Each year the verger of St. John's Church, George Cutts, waited until all the seasonal activities were over before holding a belated Christmas party in the Hall behind the Church. Over thirty guests, including six children, attended the party, among them George Cutt's thirteen-year-old nephew Peter Youngs, who remembers, ". . . Somebody had said during the evening that there was water outside in Belvedere Road. This was not uncommon as it often flooded on very high tides . . . Some time later someone else was about to leave the party early and found that the water was up to the door. At this point people began to be concerned . . .."

Though St. John's Road and Belvedere Road were flooded, the water hadn't reached the pathway between the Hall and the Church yet, so it was decided that the safest move would be to try and reach London Road South through the Church. Ernie Skipper and his wife Joyce, who were also at the party, remember, ". . . As we went through to the Church, the water was around our ankles but we managed to get about half of the people across before we realised that the front door of the Church was locked. I went back to get the key off George and as I walked out of the vestry, the water suddenly came rushing across and I was up to my chest in it, surrounded by debris and rubbish. I managed to push my way through to the School Hall and told George we needed the key. He replied, "You ain't going back there!" and when we looked the water had started to rush through the door . . .."

Back in the Church, Peter Youngs remembers, ". . . We decided to stay put . . . As the water gradually flooded the Church we had to retreat up into the choir stalls. It began to get quite frightening as we had no idea if the water was going to stop rising and we could hear the wind howling outside. Then the lights went out. Someone had some matches and we were able to light the candles on the altar. One of the elderly ladies said a prayer out loud . . .."

Mrs Herring was also at the party and was among those trapped and frightened in the School Hall, ". . . They put the ladies and the children on the stage. It wasn't high tide yet and the water was rising all the time . . .."

One of Peter Youngs' uncles, Ronnie Bennett, managed to keep the party spirit going in the School Hall by playing the piano. He kept on playing until the water was lapping round his waist and then had to give up!

Ernie Skipper continues, ". . . When the water in the School Hall reached chest level, we all had to get up onto the stage which must have been in danger of collapsing. By this time, because I had been in the water for so long, my legs were frozen and Mr Cutts' sister and another lady massaged my legs to keep them warm . . .."

With the water still rising, help had to be found and quick. Among those marooned in the Church was another of Peter Youngs' uncles, Stanley Bennett, who waded through the water to the vestry and desperately tried to ring the church bells to attract attention. Peter Youngs recalls, ". . . Unfortunately my uncle was no bellringer and failed to do it. So instead he broke a small window and hollered for help . . .." Thankfully his cries were head by a policeman, PC Leon Merrett, who was at the Mill Road corner in London Road South and wasted no time in raising the alarm that there were people trapped inside St. John's Church.

William A. Day and his wife Anne were stewards at the Yacht Club and their involvement in the rescue happened by chance. Mr Day recalls, ". . . A local fisherman, Fred Barber, had left his boat, which was damaged and sinking in the yacht basin, and taken refuge in the Yacht Club. We were having a pot of tea with him when a policeman came in and told us that there was a car near the old mortuary which was stranded in flood water. He asked if anyone had a dinghy in which we could rescue, if necessary, anyone in the car . . ..''

As yet unaware of the events at St. John's Church, Mr Day launched his own dinghy with Barber and the policeman and rowed to the car which they found had been abandoned. Mr Day continues, ". . . We rowed further down Belvedere Road to see if there was anything else we could do. Then we heard people shouting at the back of the Church and that's when we decided it must be coming from the School Hall where there were lights on . . ..'' At this point Mr Day, thinking he might be in a better position to reach or hear those trapped inside, leapt out of the boat onto what he thought was a pile of coal. ". . . It was actually just some coke floating on top of the water. I was drenched! Anyway, they shouted to us what had happened and told us that there were some people in the Church who could be in worse trouble. We rowed round to the east side of the Church and found Mr Stigles was already there in his dinghy . . ..''

It seems likely that PC Merrett, who had heard the cries from the Church, informed some firemen of the situation, who in turn were responsible for recruiting Reggie Stigles and his dinghy for the rescue effort. Mr Stigles had been to the yacht basin to check that his employer's motor boats were secure, and was on hand to help in any way he could.

After they conferred it was decided that Stigles would recover those stranded in the Church while Mr Day would help those in the School Hall. Unfortunately there were still obstacles such as the church gates which proved impossible for the dinghies to pass. However it would appear that the Belvedere Road gate was broken down by one of the many fireman in the area that night, while PC Merrett bravely dived into the water to unbolt the London Road South gate. ". . . By the time we returned this very brave policeman was extremely cold! . . ." remembers Mr Day.

Detective Constables Allenby Sparkes and R. G. Daniels managed to open the church door on London Road South, to enable the dinghy manned by Reggie Stigles, Dougie Bagshaw and Daniels himself, to enter the Church. Peter Youngs takes up the story, ". . . It was with great relief that we heard the church doors opening and then to our amazement we saw men in a small boat rowing up the aisle of the

Church! . . .." They brought the boat along to the chancel steps where Mr Youngs and the others were huddled together. In small groups they were rowed out of the Church, up Royal Thoroughfare and to the Yacht Club where Mrs Anne Day provided hot refreshments for the cold and weary rescued and rescuers. Mrs Skipper confirms, ". . . They rowed us up Parade Road, towards the Royal Hotel and the sleet was coming and the waves were rocking us about. They took us to the Yacht Club where there was a good fire going and I took my stockings off and dried my feet by it. Of course, we were all very anxious about those left in the hall . . .."

Rowing against the wind and a heavy swell, Mr Day reached the School Hall. He continues, ". . . One of the windows was removed and we began to evacuate the children and several adults. They were extremely frightened as the water had reached the stage upon which they were standing. We made about four trips back to the Yacht Club, then made a further trip to the Church itself."

Realising that the people rescued from the Church were fearful for the safety of their missing friends and relatives, he brought back a list of those still left in the School Hall. Mrs Skipper remembers, ". . . I didn't know where Ernie was, I didn't know if he had got back into the School or what had happened to him. Then they brought this list back. I was reading it down, my eyes going ahead looking for his name, and I couldn't see it! But then there it was, they put him on last, he was over the page at the bottom of the list . . .."

The rescues weren't just confined to the Church and Hall however. Ernie Skipper remembers, ". . . I was amongst the last ones left in the Hall and we could hear a little boy up St. John's Road crying for help. When Stigles came after us in his boat we told him not to bother about us, we were safe, there was a little boy who needed rescuing. So Stigles and the man who ran the Yacht Club (Mr Day) went after this little boy who was trapped in a house . . .."

As this story illustrates, throughout the night the rescuers took it in turns and swapped from boat to boat, due to the exhausting rowing and appalling weather. It is unclear exactly who manned the two dinghies that night though amongst those valiant rescuers were William Day, Reggie Stigles, Fred Barber, PC Merrett, D. C. Daniels, Dougie Bagshaw, Inspector Riddleston, PC Fiddy, Superintendent Clarke, and Divi-

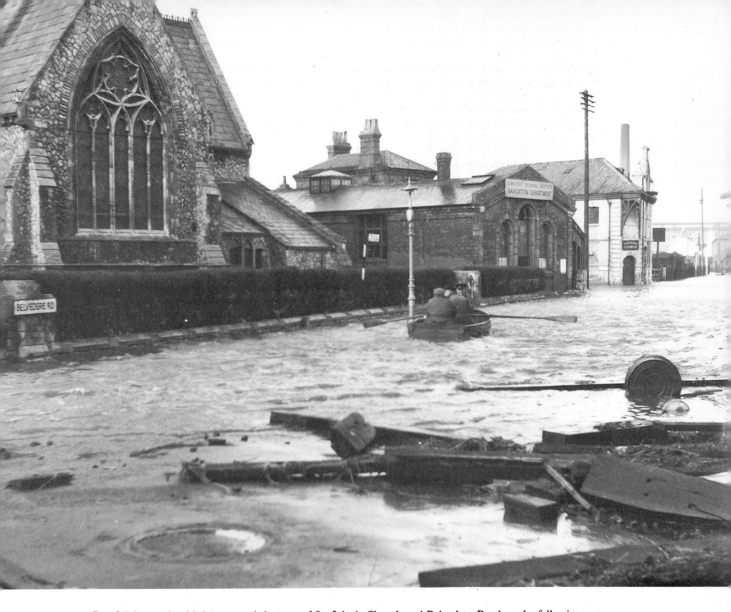

Reg Stigles rowing his boat round the area of St. John's Church and Belvedere Road on the following day. He played an important role in the St. John's Church rescue and many felt he should have received a medal for his efforts.

A small boy and his dog survey the damage and debris at the top of Belvedere Road.

sional Officer Ron Bishop. There was even a dog among the rescuers! Mr Day explains, ". . . Our brown springer spaniel *Whiskey* followed me everywhere and that night swam behind me all the time. It even followed me up the aisle of the Church!"

Eventually all the people from the Church and the Hall were rescued though when a check was made it was discovered that a ten-year-old boy was missing. Thankfully he was found at home, sitting on the doorstep, waiting for his parents to return!

Mrs Herring was another who was rescued from the Church that night. She recalls, ". . . My husband was in Commercial Road and couldn't get over the bridge so had to stay put. Eventually he managed to get through and found us at the Yacht Club. I was crying by then and he said, 'No need for you to cry now, wait till you get home and see the mess!'"

The Promenade on the morning after the flood. As the picture shows, many people came to witness the damage caused the night before.

Although the sea was still turbulent, fears of a further flooding during Sunday morning's high tide proved unfounded.

On Sunday morning the worst of the flood water had receded from the Beach Village, but the pickling plots still resembled a vast lake.

SECTION 5

Daylight

"Every time I looked out of the window," remembers Arthur Gibbs who was a virtual prisoner above his Whapload Road shop, "I saw the waves smashing against the side of the house, all the spray shooting up towards me." Like many people marooned in their own home, Mr Gibbs along with his wife, a neighbouring family and their very ill baby could only wait anxiously for the tide to recede. One rescue attempt failed as the water was too rough, although, ". . . We managed to shout a message about the baby and they said they would try and get an ambulance down in the morning."

Rescuers, such as the Rev. Peter Street of Christchurch, worked tirelessly all night. ". . . One couple and their young baby, the only residents of Eden Street, had their ground floor completely flooded. They were in the upstairs bedroom and it was difficult to rescue them. Somehow a large lorry was found and driven close to the house. A plank was dropped from the lorry to the upstairs ledge and the couple and their baby walked the plank to safety . . .."

Mr Hill was fifteen and with his family was confined in their East Street home, ". . . We stayed upstairs all night and came downstairs in the morning when the water subsided. We found everything was completely ruined, it was all covered in mud and filth as the sewers had gone. There was a tide mark six feet up the wall. This was when the horror of it really hit us and we realised how lucky we had been. There were logs stacked up outside the front door making it impossible to get out. Then we heard a voice calling out, 'Is there anybody in there?' It was the fire brigade. They worked marvellously for about an hour to get us out. Someone told us to go to the Salvation

Army. They were very good to us and gave us clean dry clothes and hot food."

Mrs J. Mitchell lived in a small cottage with her husband, brother and her widowed mother on the corner of Wildes Street and East Street. ". . . About 6 am a man in a rowing boat came round to tell us the water wouldn't get any higher. My brother was singing, *There ain't nobody here but us chickens.* The next morning my husband had to pick-a-back me out as our block of cottages was still under three feet of water. The worse thing was all our family photos and mementoes were lost or damaged as was the furniture. It took many months to get the cottage into shape again. It was a very traumatic experience for us all."

With the coming of morning it became easier to rescue those who were stranded in flooded homes or even to carry round steaming mugs of tea! "As daylight arrived we heard someone tapping on the bedroom window," remembers Doris James who was trapped upstairs at the *Kumfy Kafe*, "It was a fireman who had climbed up on the logs against the side of the house, offering us a cup of tea. It was very welcome!" Mrs James continues, ". . . Because we all had the flu, I had the fire going in the bedroom but how I wished I had some more coke or coal to keep it going . . .." Mrs James went downstairs as far as the fourth step and while she stood there the coke bucket from the front room floated out of the door, then along the hall to the bottom of the stairs. She recalls, ". . . I just bent down and picked it up out of the water, and carried it upstairs to make up the fire. What a miracle! . . . Someone must have been watching over us that night . . .."

Eventually the fireman rescued the James family and they were taken to St. Margaret's Institute in Alexandra Road, where they were reunited with all of their relations as they too were victims of the high tide. Mrs James adds, ". . . It may be forty years since the floods but I assure you it's still very vivid in my memory."

That night sixty-three homeless men, women and children were accommodated at St. Margaret's Institute and many more found refuge with friends and townspeople who gave them beds. The Christchurch Vicarage opened its doors to twenty-four people who slept on beds and floors. The Rev. Street recalls, ". . . One man, drunk on the Saturday night, was brought to the Vicarage, and found a bed. The following morning he said

Firemen check the safety of Whapload Road residents. The police station now stands here.

at breakfast, 'Could I have my wife back tonight please, the lady I slept with wasn't my wife!' . . .."

Mr R. R. Davis, officer of the Civil Defence Organisation, was put in charge of the relief side of the work on Sunday morning, though when he arrived he found rest centres had already been established by the Women's Voluntary Service, one of the first welfare services on the scene. Its members worked long hours during that night and early morning, preparing hot soup and tea for all the flood victims and rescuers. The Scouts meanwhile acted as messengers, rescued people in boats, helped at the rest centres and cleared debris the next day. Among the many on hand were the Salvation Army and the Territorial Army, along with many members of the public who offered to help.

". . . People were coming down with their ordinary clothes on, no rubber boots, and wading in waist deep to piggy-back others out or to take in hot tea and sandwiches," remembered Gus Jensen, "They didn't seem to bother how wet they got as long as they could be of some help."

There were fears that there would be a repetition of the flooding during the morning's high tide. Fortunately however, the wind had died down and although the water rose at Lowestoft Bridge to around twenty-three feet, there was no further trouble. Mr Arthur Gibbs recalls, ". . . On Sunday morning we couldn't see the sea wall, there was only water. Then we began to see something dark, gradually emerging as the tide went down — it was the sea wall. It hadn't broken, the sea had gone right over it! We all started to clear the debris that blocked the stairs and just as we got through the ambulance pulled up. The baby was diagnosed as having pneumonia and was rushed to hospital . . .."

By morning the Rev. Peter Street was tired and filthy, having worked all night. He remembers standing on the back of a lorry travelling up the High Street and seeing members of his congregation walking to the Church, completely unaware of the flood. ". . . I was quite surprised when I realised it was already time for morning service, and there was even more surprise on their faces at seeing their Vicar standing on the back of a lorry, as black as a coalman!"

With around eighty percent of the Christchurch parish flooded, the sea wall

Christchurch played an important role during the 1953 flood, with the Reverend Peter Street actively involved in many rescues that night.

Anguish Street, the Beach Village. A policeman lifts his coat tails to continue his beat. The flood weakened many of the houses in this area and although many were re-plastered, the salt soon came through again. Many people had spent their last night in the Village.

undoubtedly saved lives. The £300,000 that the Town had invested in the wall since the War proved to be worthwhile and the Borough Surveyor, Mr Gentry, pointed out that the devastation would have been worse had the wall not been there to intercept the surge.

". . . When the flood started to subside in the morning," recalls Mrs Tuck, "my husband put his thigh boots on and piggy-backed us through the water. A Mr Capps Jenner took us to his house in Spurgeon Score where his wife made us a most welcome hot drink. Then my sister, who lived in Kirkley, came and picked us up. We stayed there for the night though my husband stopped behind to start cleaning up the mess. What a sight it was when we got home! There was thick mud on the floor . . .."

Russell Graves worked for Fred Newson who lived at Dean Lodge on Whapload Road, where his workshops for boatbuilding were also sited. Two boats which were almost finished had been washed away in the floods and ended up on the banks below Arnold House. He remembers, ". . . We had to get rid of about ten inches of mud and sewage before we could put them back inside the workshop . . .."

Mr Gibbs remembers, ". . . We found a big cod sitting in the arm-chair, which had been thrown against the wall. My wife had put one of my shirts on the back of a chair, to dry near the fire. It had gone up the chimney, shirt and all! The sash windows were hanging on their cords, swinging like pub signs, and the waves had even smashed the lamp shades . . .."

Butter and margarine was swept from the shop by the waves and smeared over the walls of the house next door where Jimmy Grimmer lived with his brothers and parents. Mr Grimmer says, ". . . All our furniture was swept away. The hanging bowls in the ceiling were full of water, the old fireplace in the front room had fallen out of the wall. They chipped all the plaster off the walls, back to the soft brick and re-plastered but the salt came through again . . . We never went back."

Thomas Hurn's father was a fisherman, born in the Beach Village. He recalls, ". . . The fishermen's cottages were flooded and my Mum and Dad had to come over to ours for six months. They went home for two months and then they had to come again for six months. The cottage was all brick, and had started to collapse . . .."

Mrs Mann was devastated when she saw the wreckage of her Cumberland Square

Watson's breakdown truck outside the Steam Laundry which was owned by the same company. The breakdown truck itself became waterlogged and had to be towed out by an ex-army vehicle owned by Mr Cleveland.

home. ". . . It was heartbreaking as we had worked and worked for our new dining room suite. We couldn't do anything, there was salt pouring out of the walls, you couldn't have anything on the floors or use electricity. We had to live with mother for three months but when we went back we were so frightened that we had floodboards made. We even kept most of the furniture upstairs! If someone came round, we had to go upstairs for a chair. We stayed there a year after that but we were so frightened, we had to leave."

Russell Graves remembers that his employer Fred Newson also lost a lot from his Whapload Road workshops, ". . . We spent that Sunday morning rowing about the gasworks to see if we could find anything that belonged to us. We had a terrific amount of wood about the place that just got washed away. We never found half of it. Of course, Mr Newson's house was just as bad as the workshop . . .."

Mrs Barbara Buckingham née Stone worked at the Gorrock Rope Works also situated in Whapload Road. She recalls, ". . . I was appalled at the destruction the flood had caused. The tarpit (this was used for the nets) had water in it and bales of twine had crashed into the houses next door . . .."

Mr Gibbs lost most of his shop's stock in the flood, ". . . We picked up all the tins and cleaned them up, stacking them upstairs till we opened again. I had already sent my list in of what we had lost when we found that the tins had all turned red rusty. I had to dump the lot of them! There were two lorry loads! And the salt is still coming out of the walls to this day." He also suffered from an ugly side effect of the flood, looting, which sadly took place around the town over that weekend. With so many premises empty, it was easy for heartless thieves to take what they wanted. Mr Gibbs recalls, "We went up to my mother-in-law's house that Sunday night to have some dinner and when we came back the shop had been stripped bare. Anything that could be saved was gone. Jars of sweets, everything . . .."

The Rev. Street tells the tale of a man who tried to cheat inspectors who came to assess the damage to his home by painting a false line on the wall of his downstairs rooms to indicate the height of the water. However, he adds, ". . . Many people of course were the opposite and had to be pressured to take money or help . . .." The Rev. Street remembers, "Through the agony and damage caused to many homes we were able to bring Christian help to many people. Some of the fisher folk helped and members of the congregation also gave many hours of their time. The flood brought people together in the weeks following as never before.''

Gus Jensen admits, ''. . . We had a lot of help from the officials. The Health Department dried the houses. Everyone worked hard, the Town Clerk, Harry Cormack and his team from the Health Department, the Borough Surveyor, the Highway Superintendent. If it hadn't been for them we would have been in a lot of trouble with disease as a result of the flooding and its damage . . ..''

Help came from all quarters. The town's grocers gave soup, tinned meat and vegetables which provided over one hundred people with a Sunday lunch, with a further hundred and fifty meals served that evening.

The loss of food during the flood posed an immediate problem and compensation of thirty shillings was soon made available. The National Assistance Board sent Cyril Snelling and a colleague to Christchurch Hall where they spent all day taking claims and making cash payments to residents of the Beach Village.

Whereas a few people did abuse the National Assistance compensation schemes and as a result carpets appeared in homes where there was lino before, not everyone benefitted. Mrs Crowe, now of Haward Street, lived at the bottom of London Road in the premises currently occupied by Victoria Insurance. She recalls, ''We had bare boards for weeks and weeks, no electricity, no gas, and received no compensation.''

One man remembers hearing a woman relating a rather dubious story about how she had lost all her furniture. ''It wasn't very good furniture,'' the woman said, ''and the water melted the glue. It all fell to bits and floated under the door!''

''. . . It reminded me of during the War,'' says Peter Hemsley, who lived in London Road South at the time. ''After every bombing raid people would come down the town and have a look at the damage. That next morning after the flood, you should have seen the number of people who were trying to force their way into our property! I remember saying, 'And what can I do for you ladies?' They replied, 'We've come to have a look around!' I said, 'Not likely!' ''

He continues, ''. . . I came home that Monday or Tuesday night, and was suddenly told, 'Stand still! You're under arrest!' It was a police officer! He told me I was

London Road South, looking down towards the bridge. Many houses in this area were flooded and their residents re-housed or found shelter elsewhere.

The flood seemed to cause damage all over the town. The Promenade was broken and there was also damage caused to the parks and gardens on the sea front by the salt water inundation.

trespassing and this area had been evacuated. 'I live here!' I replied. There were only a few people near us who hadn't been evacuated. They thought I was a burglar!" He adds, ". . . We had the RAF driers in, and when they stripped the wallpaper they found the mark of the 1900's floods. They reckoned that a big flood occurs every fifty years . . ."

Perhaps one of the flood's most unfortunate victims was Terence Palmer. He had been married about a year and had just paid a year's rent in advance on a house directly opposite Christchurch Green. He recalls, "We had some carpets put down that Saturday afternoon, and we went in at four o'clock. That evening we were having a drink with the man who owned the place and a lady from a nearby house came running in and told us that the floods were here! When we looked outside the water was flowing round the buildings. It was the first we knew about it . . .." Mr Palmer's new home was devastated. ". . . We had a telegraph pole come right in our back yard and through the kitchen window but they had to cut it into four to get it out again! The RAF driers came in to dry the place and the Canadian Red Cross gave us a carpet. We also got food parcels. We lost all our furniture which rotted and even after we decorated again, the salt wouldn't stop coming out of the walls. We never moved in."

Some were luckier though. Mr Hill's family lived next to the corner shop in East Street and were able to move straight away into a house in Factory Street which his father had previously bought. "We were much more fortunate than a lot of people who lost a great deal. Truly, this was the end of life in the Beach Village . . .."

However, Gus Jensen argues that it needn't have been. ". . . The Beach could have overcome it quite easily. It started off as slum clearance in the forties then the flood happened. Now they would just get improvement grants but there was no money to rebuild then. They could have but they didn't . . .."

The Beach Village never recovered. Disheartened and fearful of further flooding, many families never moved back and within ten years the area had been cleared and given over to industry, leaving the town without one remaining example of Beach Village life.

Elsewhere in the town, the Suffolk Hotel remained without boilers, gas or electricity and with a layer of mud covering the ground floor. Twelve resident guests insisted on

The Fire Brigade pump out the cellar at Coles the chemist in London Road North. When they pumped out the Suffolk Hotel they found the body of the hotel cat, which had drowned. The manager Mr Smith, had been unable to coax it out on the Saturday night.

staying and for dinner were served roast chicken, carrots, potatoes and green peas, all cooked over the dining room fire. "With the candles we had bought to light the rooms it looked like a gypsy encampment," said the hotel manager, Mr Smith.

On Monday the fire brigade started to drain the water out of the cellars and it was possible to see what remained down there. Amongst the debris was coke which had floated from the store and precious glass which was completely shattered. Also found was Mr Smith's drowned cat, which he had been unable to coax out on Sunday night. The damage in the food store alone was estimated at hundreds of pounds with the contents of a newly-opened case of tea marking the high water level. Coloured vermicelli, usually put on ice cream, decorated the walls while sugar had dissolved from its cartons. By Monday night however, the hotel was full of commercial travellers as usual.

Firemen from all over the country came to the town to help. Here, firemen from Bristol start to pump out the low area around the swimming pool and yacht pond. Lowestoft lighthouse can be seen in the background.

It took a while for the town to recover from the full effects of the flooding. In some areas there was no gas supply for three weeks, "... We were the only ones in Haward Street with any cooking facilities," remembers Mrs Cullen, "As we had an old stove, we were cooking for the whole road!"

The Mayor of Lowestoft, Mr W. H. B. Sanders, paid tribute to those who had helped, "... Throughout, the willing assistance of a very large number of people too numerous to mention by name has been an enormous help and the very high morale has been generally maintained by the victims of the flood and the cheerfulness with which they faced their ordeal was something of which we can be well proud. We in Lowestoft have suffered grievous damage to, and loss of, property but we have been spared the tragic loss of life which has occurred in so many other areas ...."

Without the massive media coverage that it would be given today, many were unaware of the flood until the news broke next day. Even those who lived on the outskirts of town were unaware of the happenings that were taking place that night. Sodden up to his chest, Mr Dalley finally arrived home at Carlton Colville after a traumatic night. He had been conductor on one of the buses that drove over the flooded bridge, waded waist deep in water and cycled home in a howling wind. "I'm wet through," he told his wife as he entered the house.

"Is it raining?" she replied innocently.

The four men from Lowestoft who received flood awards. Left to right, Mr A. T. F. Jensen received the BEM, Fireman J. Roach received the Queen's Commendation, Leading Fireman Barlow also received the BEM, while Mr J. G. Crooks received the Queen's Commendation. Mr Crooks received his medal in recognition of his work during the flood at the Gas Works where he was General Foreman.

Barclays Bank was situated on the corner of London Road and Commercial Road. Staff started to clean up the premises on Sunday morning, determined to have the bank open as usual on the following day. Standing on the left is Jimmy Banham, kneeling beside him is Roger Parker, standing on the right is Mr Neville Coe and bending down is Mr Parker's brother.

By Monday morning the corporation workmen had started to repair the cliffs just below the Cliff Road area. Hundreds of tons of ballast were used in this rebuilding operation.

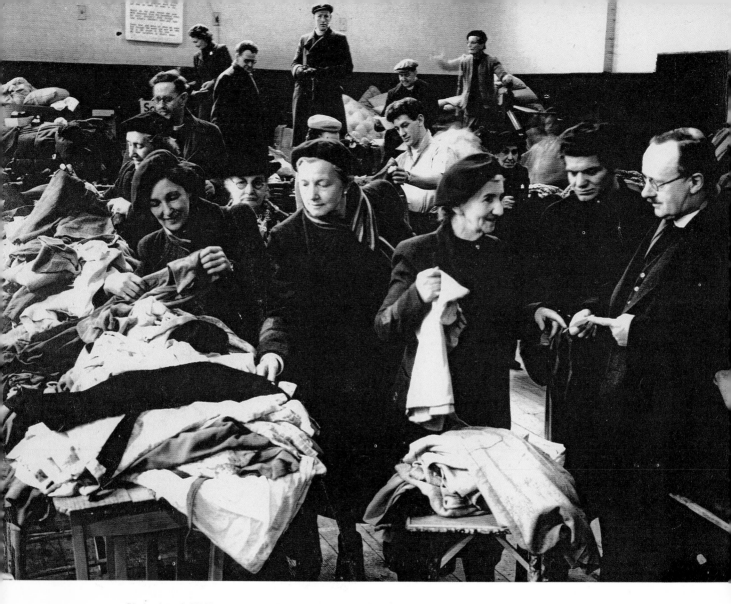

Christchurch Hall was opened the next day to provide food and clothing for flood victims. In the picture some of the members of the W.V.S. can be seen preparing and sorting through the clothes. The lady at the front holding the piece of white clothing was Mrs Ollington, the W.V.S. organiser while on her left is Mrs Woodgreaves, Miss Williams and Mrs Back.